How to Manage Your Money

LIFE SKILLS

How to Manage Your Money

HERON BOOKS

Published by
Heron Books, Inc.
20950 SW Rock Creek Road
Sheridan, OR 97378

heronbooks.com

Special thanks to all the teachers and students who
provided feedback instrumental to this edition.

Third Edition © 1976, 2023 Heron Books
All Rights Reserved

ISBN: 978-0-89-739335-5

Any unauthorized copying, translation, duplication or distribution, in whole or in part, by any means, including electronic copying, storage or transmission, is a violation of applicable laws.

The Heron Books name and the heron bird symbol are registered trademarks
of Delphi Schools, Inc.

6 March 2023

At Heron Books, we think learning should be engaging and fun. It should be hands-on and allow students to move at their own pace.

To facilitate this we have created a learning guide that will help any student progress through this book, chapter by chapter, with confidence and interest.

Get learning guides at
heronbooks.com/learningguides.

For teacher resources,
such as a final exam, email
teacherresources@heronbooks.com.

We would love to hear from you!
Email us at *feedback@heronbooks.com*.

CONTENTS

CHAPTER 1
What *Is* Money? 3

CHAPTER 2
Making a Budget 7
    Creating a Budget 7
    Tips 10
    Takeaways 11
    What Can Go Wrong? 12
    Seems Like A Lot of Work 14

CHAPTER 3
Budgeting Practice 17

CHAPTER 4
Savings and Interest 21
    Savings 21
    Interest 23
    Risk 24
    Inflation 25
    Summary 26

CHAPTER 5
Checking Accounts 29
    How Do Checks Work? 30
    Deposits 32

CHAPTER 6
Bank Statements and Reconciliation 35
    Bank Statement 35
    Reconciliation 37
    Errors That Can Affect Reconciliation 40

CHAPTER 7
Reconciliation Practice 43

CHAPTER 8
Online Banking 51

CHAPTER 9
Debit and Credit Cards 55
    Debit Card. 55
    Credit Card 56

CHAPTER 10
You Decide 61

CHAPTER 1

What *Is* Money?

CHAPTER 1

What *Is* Money?

People have always needed and wanted the goods or services of others. Early on, people traded something they had for something they wanted--a cow for grain, fabric for a pan, work for a meal.

Paper and metal coins eventually took the place of one side of the bargain because people agreed that the paper and metal coins stood for something of value. And now, there is even a digital form of money that is used on a computer network. All of these things are ways to exchange something one has for something one wants.

So, what is money? **Money** is simply something people agree has value. It can be exchanged more easily than objects for the things they want to do and have.

And the simplicity is that you want to have more money than you need, not less.

CHAPTER 2

Making a Budget

CHAPTER 2

Making a Budget

A **budget** is a listing of income (money earned) and expenses (things you spend money on), both expected and actual. You can use a budget to keep track of the money you earn and spend so that you don't spend more than you make. And, ideally, you make more than you spend!

CREATING A BUDGET

There are many ways to create a budget but they all involve the same principle of keeping track of income and expenses.

Here is a sample budget for one month that is easy to put together and follow.

PROPOSED BUDGET FOR JULY

Money at the beginning of the month:

    Savings bank account: $500

    Money in wallet (cash): $28

    Total money: $528

MAKING A BUDGET

Income:

	Planned	Actual
Allowance earned	$ 40	_____
Part-time job	100	_____
Misc.	0	_____
Total	$140	_____

Expenses:

	Planned	Actual
Entertainment	$30	_____
Gas	20	_____
Gifts	20	_____
Snacks	20	_____
Savings	30	_____
Misc.	20	_____
Total	$140	_____

You can now use the amounts you've put down to manage your earnings and expenditures (expenses) throughout the month. It helps keep you on track so you end up with more money at the end of the month than you've spent.

At the end of the month, you can fill out the "Actual" column, like this:

Income:

	Planned	Actual	
Allowance earned	$ 40	$ 40	
Part-time job	100	105	
Misc.	0	5	(a friend paid back a loan)
Total	$140	$150	

MAKING A BUDGET

Expenses:

	Planned	Actual
Entertainment	$30	$25
Gas	20	15
Gifts	20	22
Snacks	20	24
Savings	30	30
Misc.	20	22
Total	$140	$138

Money at the end of the month:

Savings account:	$530
Money in wallet (cash):	$10
Total money:	$540

This was a successful budget. At the end of the month, you have more money than you started with. And you can then set your August budget using your new total money figure.

Here is an example of the same budget that wasn't so successful.

Income:

	Planned	Actual	
Allowance earned	$ 40	$ 25	
Part-time job	100	105	
Misc.	0	5	(a friend paid back a loan)
Total	$140	$135	

MAKING A BUDGET

<u>Expenses</u>:

	Planned	Actual
Entertainment	$30	$40
Gas	20	15
Gifts	20	22
Snacks	20	28
Savings	30	10
Misc.	20	35
Total	$140	$150

<u>Money at the end of the month</u>:

Savings account: $510

Money in wallet (cash): $3

Total money: $513

In this example, you have spent more money than you made. If you keep that up, you'll end up broke. You have to reduce expenses and/or make more money.

TIPS

Here are some tips in putting together and following a budget. Notice their use in the examples:

1. All amounts are rounded off to the nearest dollar.

2. You need a way of covering things you didn't predict would happen, so there is a miscellaneous listing for both income and expenses. Generally, you want to keep these amounts minor, so your overall budget can work.

3. To keep track of your expenses, you can get receipts for everything you buy and keep them, or keep a running list of them. Then, at the end of the month, separate them into the categories in your budget, add them up, and enter the totals.

4. Check your calculations by comparing them to the money you have in the bank and in your wallet to make sure they are right.

5. You can always check your budget figures in this way:

   total money at the beginning of the month

   + income

   – expenditures

   = total money at the end of the month

TAKEAWAYS

Once you have filled out your budget at the end of the month, you can see how well you are doing at making good financial decisions. If you are spending more money than you make, figure out how to reduce expenses and/or make more money.

Using the unsuccessful sample budget, here are some possible ideas for how to make more money:

a) Allowance. Figure out why you only got $25 instead of the $40 you predicted. Figure out how to earn more next month.

b) Part-time job: Is there any way to raise this another $5 for next month?

c) Miscellaneous: Does anyone else owe you money? Do you have anything you don't need that you can sell?

Here are some possible ways to reduce expenditures:

a) You spent more than your allocation for entertainment (**allocation** is the amount of money allowed for a given area of spending). You can figure out some cheaper entertainment for the next month.

MAKING A BUDGET

b) You overspent the snacks allocation by quite a bit. Maybe you could cut this down by not carrying very much cash around, so you won't spend it on snacks.

c) Miscellaneous was very high. Again, maybe if you don't carry much cash, you won't spend it on things unplanned for.

d) If you'd put more money in savings, you would probably have had more total money at the end of the month. Maybe next month you can put your budgeted amount of money into savings as early as possible in the month, so that it won't get spent on other things.

WHAT CAN GO WRONG?

As you see, a well-kept budget gives you a way of controlling your money and doing what you want to do with it.

One possible problem you can have with this is how to keep track of all the expenditures. Of course, sometimes you don't get receipts for what you buy, as with vending machines. A little notebook can help keep track of those expenditures; there are also apps for your phone that do this.

Here's an example showing where your budget doesn't balance, and how you then need to adjust it.

Money at beginning of the month:

    Savings account: $500

    Money in wallet: $28

    Total money: $528

MAKING A BUDGET

Suppose you get to the end of July, and you count your total money, receipts and income, and it looks like this:

Income:

	Planned	Actual	
Allowance earned	$40	$25	
Part-time job	100	105	
Misc.	0	5	(a friend paid back a loan)
Total	$140	$135	

Expenses:

	Planned	Actual
Entertainment	$30	$40
Transportation	20	15
Gifts	20	22
Snacks	20	28
Savings	30	10
Misc.	20	15
Total	$140	$130

Money at the end of the month:

    Money in savings account: $510

    Money in wallet: $3

    Total money: $513

According to this budget, you earned $135 and only spent $130, which means you should have $5 more at the end of the month than you had at the beginning. But you've counted everything up, and you actually have $15 less! This means you must have spent $20 somewhere that you didn't keep track of, so you have to add that to the miscellaneous spent amount.

13

MAKING A BUDGET

Since this now makes your miscellaneous $35, which is way over the allocation, you might decide to be much more careful about keeping track of miscellaneous expenditures next month so that you can see where this money is going and control it better. This might get you back to keeping receipts or a notebook.

SEEMS LIKE A LOT OF WORK

When you have a lot of income and not many expenses, it can seem like a budget isn't very important. But, even so, by keeping a budget, you might find that you end up saving a lot *more* money for something you'd really like to have, instead of spending it on things that aren't really very important to you.

When your income is nearly the same as your expenses, a budget becomes very important to keep you out of debt and enable you to accumulate any savings at all. It will also help you find ways to make more income.

And when your income is less than your expenses, a budget may be your only hope of getting back into control of your money.

Whichever scenario is yours, the small amount of time spent planning and following a budget will help put you in control of your finances, and ideally keep you making more money than you spend.

CHAPTER 3

Budgeting Practice

CHAPTER 3

Budgeting Practice

Here is a scenario you can use to practice your budgeting skill. Smaller numbers are used in the examples to make it a bit easier to do.

Fisk L. Prudence had $1,344.56 in his savings account at the beginning of the month, $89.76 in his checking account, and $23.40 cash.

He expected income during the month of $250 from a part-time job and $30 owed him by a friend. (He works around the house to earn room and board from his parents, but no money is exchanged for that.)

He planned to spend about $15 each weekend for entertainment (movies and restaurants), $10 a week for gas, $40 on a tune-up for his car, $50 for a new pair of shoes, and $20 on other things. (There will be 4 weekends in this next month.) He wanted to put $15 into his checking account toward an insurance payment on his car that will be due later, and whatever was left over into savings.

1. Write the budget that Fisk would write at the beginning of the month.

At the end of the month, Fisk has $1,384.56 in his savings account, $99.76 in his checking account, and $22.34 cash. He has stubs from his paychecks that show that he earned $261.20, and his friend paid him back $20.

BUDGETING PRACTICE

He has the following receipts:

Gas $10, Movies $12; Restaurant $35; Gas $5; Shoes $45.56; Movies $12; Car tune-up $42.50; Gas $15; restaurant $23.

2. Re-copy the budget Fisk did at the beginning of the month and fill in the actual income and expenditures columns. Notice that he did make deposits into his checking account and savings accounts, and how much they were. You will have to compute what his miscellaneous expenditures must have been.

3. Evaluate how well Fisk did during the month on his budget, and make suggestions as to how he could do better the next month.

4. Make up a possible budget for Fisk for the beginning of the next month.

5. Make up Fisk's "actual" income and expenditure figures for the next month and fill in his end-of-month figures.

CHAPTER 4

Savings and Interest

CHAPTER 4

Savings and Interest

SAVINGS

There are a lot of ways to keep and store money for future needs, emergencies or periods of low income. You can keep a certain amount in your checking account that you never spend. You could even store cash in a safe place in your home.

But there are ways to use the money you are saving to make *more* money.

There are many institutions that will pay for the use of someone else's money. This is called **interest**.

Here is a simple example of how interest works. You (and many, many other people) deposit money in a savings account in a bank. The bank holds some of the money and loans out the rest. From the loans, the bank earns interest—money the borrowers pay the bank for the use of the loaned money. Part of this goes to you as interest on your deposit, and the rest the bank keeps for operating expenses and profit.

There are different institutions and different ways to make money from your savings. All have advantages and disadvantages you need to examine in order to decide what is right for you.

SAVINGS AND INTEREST

Here are some examples:

A credit union is much like a bank, but it may pay you for the use of your money in another way. Every **quarter**, three months or one-fourth of a year, the money earned by the credit union from those who borrow from it is divided up among those who have money in their savings accounts. These are called **dividends** (from the word *divide*). Thus, you receive a percentage of the profits.

Both banks and credit unions also offer **certificates of deposit**. The way these work is you give them a certain amount of money for a specific amount of time. When the time is up (called the **maturity date**), you get your money back (called the **principal**) and you also get an agreed-upon amount of interest. The amount of interest will normally be higher than a savings account because the bank can depend on having your money available for that amount of time. And generally speaking, the longer you wait, the more interest you get.

Bonds work similarly to certificates of deposits, but they are offered by companies and governments. You give them a certain amount of money for a specific amount of time, and on the maturity date, you get an agreed-upon amount of interest.

Insurance companies also offer policies that can sometimes pay dividends.

Another way to try to earn from your savings is to buy stock. Many companies make money by dividing an interest in the company into pieces called **shares**. All the pieces together are call **stock**. Companies sell shares of stock, and people who think the company will grow, buy one or many shares, and then have part ownership of the company. The company uses the money from sales of stock to expand its business.

If a company is successful and makes more profits, the value of the shares people own rises. And some stocks pay dividends based on the company's profits, much the way credit unions do. So, if you own $100 worth of stock in a company paying dividends, and the company made a profit, an additional amount of money will show up in your account on a set timeline—such as quarterly. Now, instead of $100, you might have $102.

You can hold the stocks to earn dividends or sell the stocks if you want your money back. There is an element of risk here. If the stock price went down, you might not be able to get all your money back.

For example, say you bought 10 shares of Sal's Cupcake Factory stock for $10 a share (costing you $100). Over time, the value of those shares increased until they were worth $20 a share—selling at this point would give you $200, with $100 of that being profit. But just as you were about to sell, the company was no longer able to get flour and couldn't make cupcakes, causing its stock value to drop to $2 a share. Selling now would not give you any profit—in fact, you would lose $8 a share, or $80 of your initial investment.

INTEREST

Let's return to banks and the subject of interest. The interest paid to you by a bank is figured as a percentage of the money you have in savings, which is computed and added to your savings at regular intervals of time.

For example, a bank may advertise 4% interest yearly. If you have $200 in savings for one year, then at the end of that year the bank adds in another 4% of $200, which is $8 (0.04 × $200 = $8), and you have $208. The percentage used to calculate interest is called the **interest rate**. And again, the initial savings amount is called the **principal**.

It makes a difference how often the bank computes your interest. Suppose in the example above that your interest on the $200 savings was computed every 6 months instead of yearly. Remember that the interest rate is 4% each year—that doesn't change. At the end of 6 months, the bank pays you 4% × $200 × .5, since the money has been in for ½ year. This is $4. You now have $204 in savings. This is your new principal. At the end of another 6 months, interest is again computed: 4% × $204 × .5 = $4.08. You now have $208.08 in savings—an extra $0.08 resulting from the fact that interest was computed more often. If the bank computed your interest every month, it would result in a bit more interest paid.

SAVINGS AND INTEREST

This action of computing interest on top of other interest is called **compounding the interest.** You may see it stated like this in advertisements: 6% interest, compounded quarterly. This would be an interest rate of 6% per year, computed every three months. As the example shows, the more frequently the interest is compounded, the more interest you earn.

Obviously, the total amount of interest you get on savings depends on how long you leave the money there.

RISK

All methods of saving have *some* risk. Here are a few examples.

- If you decided not to trust anyone else with your money and saved it in your house, guarding it yourself, it could get lost or stolen (and it wouldn't earn any interest).

- If you put your money in a bank or a credit union, and too many people who borrowed money from the bank or credit union were unable to repay the money, the bank could go bankrupt (having less money than it owes to people) and you could lose your savings as well.

- If you buy stock in a company and the company goes out of business, the stock might become worthless.

Generally speaking, the safer your money is, the less it will earn. This is because the safeguards cost money, and people are usually willing to take some risks only if they have a chance to make more money that way.

Here is an example of a safeguard that has been put in place for banks and credit unions.

In banks, your savings are automatically insured against loss up to a certain amount by an independent federal agency called the Federal Deposit Insurance Corporation (FDIC). Banks pay for this insurance from their earnings, and clearly state whether they are FDIC-insured. If the bank goes bankrupt, the

SAVINGS AND INTEREST

FDIC will give the depositors back their money up to $250,000. There is a similar insurance policy for credit unions through the National Credit Union Association (NCUA).

So, if you use a bank or credit union for your savings, your money is safer, but you will generally get a lower interest rate.

INFLATION

There's one other thing to be aware of when saving your money. When certain conditions occur in a country, money becomes worth less. This is called **inflation**, and an inflation rate of 10%, for example, means that each year it takes about 10% more money to buy the same thing. For example, if a loaf of bread cost $1.00 in the United States one year, and there was a national inflation rate of 10%, it would likely cost $1.10 the next year.

What does inflation have to do with savings? Just this: If you have your money in a savings account at, say, 8% interest and inflation is 10%, then the $100 you put into savings at the beginning of the year will be $108 at the end of the year. But by that time, it takes $110 to buy what you could have bought for $100. So, you've actually lost buying power. Of course, you haven't lost as much as if you hadn't been earning any interest on your money at all. But you can see that inflation acts to reduce the value of saving.

It is important to find a way of saving that makes more return than inflation is taking away. If you were earning 10% interest and inflation was 6%, you would be gaining about 4% in buying power.

You can also try to make your money earn money by buying things with it that you can later hope to sell at a profit. Some people buy real estate, gold or works of art that they think will gain in value (or at least keep up with inflation) as a way to save their money. Buying stocks in the hope that their value will rise, as opposed to buying them for the dividends, is another way to do this.

Or you can buy an insurance policy that is guaranteed to pay you back a certain amount under certain conditions.

SAVINGS AND INTEREST

Not all these ways of saving money pay regular interest. But all of them can be looked at *as if* that were the case, by comparing the initial investment and the eventual return and computing the rate of gain. Then you can judge whether the rate of return on your savings justifies the risk.

SUMMARY

To summarize:

1. One saves in order to store and accumulate money for future needs and wants, emergencies or periods of low income.

2. There are different ways to save, and grow, money including putting it in banks, credit unions, bonds, stocks, real estate and insurance.

3. To compare one method of saving to another, consider the rate of interest and the method by which it is computed, and the safety of your money.

4. The safer your money is, the less it will earn.

5. Inflation acts to reduce the value of money that is saved, so you need to earn more than the rate of inflation if you want to increase your buying power.

CHAPTER 5

Checking Accounts

CHAPTER 5

Checking Accounts

As you begin to have more income and expenses, the need arises for some way to store money and pay bills that doesn't involve walking around with wads of cash and bags of coins in a purse or pocket. The first system for safely storing and tracking money and goods was established in Ancient Rome, and over centuries it has evolved to become the modern checking account.

A **checking account** is an account set up at a bank or other financial institution for depositing and storing money, and then accessing it to pay bills and cover expenses. There are different types of checking accounts, such as personal, business, and student.

The bank keeps track of all the money going into and out of the account. Once a month, the bank sends you this accounting, which is called a **bank statement**.

There are various ways you can interact with your checking account. You can access it online with a computer or an app, and make deposits and pay bills this way. You can use paper checks. Or you can use both. It's important to understand both because most people and businesses use both.

Online banking will be covered in a later chapter. First, we will familiarize you with handling a checking account using paper checks. But many of these principles also apply when you are handling your account mostly online.

CHECKING ACCOUNTS

HOW DO CHECKS WORK?

A **check** is a written order to a bank to pay a certain amount from money in your account. Blank checks come together in a **checkbook**.

If you have a checking account with money in it, you can write a check.

When you write a check, money goes out.

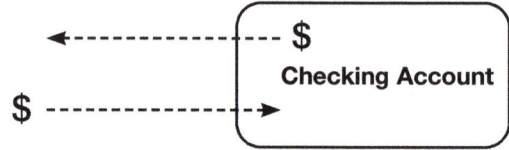

When you make a deposit, money goes in.

On the check appears the name of the bank where the account is, and the name and address of the person paying the money (the account holder).

There are spaces to fill in the date, the amount of the check, the person or business to whom the money is going, the account holder's signature line, and any note they might want to make about the check.

In the top right corner, there is a check number to help you keep track of checks written. The numbers just below it are used to identify the bank itself. The numbers on the bottom of the check include the number the bank uses to identify the specific account, and other tracking numbers used by the bank.

You can see all these things on the sample check that follows.

CHECKING ACCOUNTS

```
No. 141  $_____           JOHN DOE                                              141
Date_____ 20 ___        JANE DOE                                       12-121/5555
To:_____           123 Maple Dr.
_____            Elmville, MA 13579                     _____, 20__

For:_____
_____            Pay to the
                            Order of_____$_____
Bal For'd  _____           _____DOLLARS
Amt Dep.   _____              BANK OF MASSACHUSETTS
Total      _____              Elmville, Massachusetts
This check _____           Memo_____                            _____
New Bal    _____           *"13141592654*  :2201413340455

      stub                         check
```

After you fill out the check, you separate it from the check stub, which stays in your checkbook (see above). The **check stub** helps you keep track of all the checks you have written, and how much is currently in your account.

The check stub has the number of the check (so that you can easily see which check this stub refers to), the date, who the check is paid to, and for what.

"Bal For'd" (Balance Forward) means how much money was left after the last check you wrote. "Amt Dep." (Amount Deposited) is for any money you've put into the account since the last time you wrote a check.

You add these to get the total in your account, then enter the amount of this check and subtract to get the New Balance ("New Bal").

All checks don't have stubs, but there is always a place to put the information that goes on the stub of checks. Sometimes a copy is made as you write a check and when the check is removed, it remains in the checkbook as a record.

When you get your checkbook, look for the stub or the place where you keep track of the money coming in and going out.

CHECKING ACCOUNTS

Here's the way a stub and check might look when filled out. In this case, John Doe had $127.50 left after the last check he wrote. He made no deposits since then.

```
No. 141  $   49.75           JOHN DOE                                                 141
Date June 9  20 23           JANE DOE                                         12-121/5555
To:   Tom's Bikes            123 Maple Dr.                          June 9    20 23
                             Elmville, MA 13579
For:  B's B'day
      bicycle helmet         Pay to the
                             Order of    Tom's Bikes                           $ 49.75
Bal For'd    127 50              Forty-nine and 75/100-------------------------- DOLLARS
Amt Dep.        -                BANK OF MASSACHUSETTS
Total        127 50              Elmville, Massachusetts
This check    49 75          Memo    B's Birthday                          (signature)
New Bal       77 75          *"13141592654*   :2201413340455
```

DEPOSITS

You use a **deposit slip** to make a deposit (you can get them at the bank or some may come with your checks).

On the deposit slip, you put down the date, identify the account that the money is going into, and state how much money you are putting in.

If you are depositing a check, such as a paycheck, you need to **endorse** (sign your name to) the check. This tells the bank that you are the person the check is made out to, and you agree to cash or deposit it. There is a space given for this on the back of the check and you sign in pen in the same way your name is shown on the front. (Businesses often have inked rubber stamps that are used to endorse checks going into the business account.)

When you deposit money, the bank gives you a receipt showing the amount you deposited at that time. It is a good idea to keep these receipts until you receive your bank statement each month. Again, a bank statement is a listing of your account activity sent by your bank.

CHAPTER 6

Bank Statements and Reconciliation

CHAPTER 6

Bank Statements and Reconciliation

BANK STATEMENT

This is an example of a bank statement for a checking account:

BANK OF MASSACHUSETTS

Statement of Account

John Doe	Bank of Massachusetts
Jane Doe	777 E. 7th Street
123 Maple Dr.	Elmville, MA 13578
Elmville, MA 13579	(508) 876-5432

SUMMARY OF CHECKING ACCOUNT 3340455

Beginning Balance as of	05/15/23	$376.40
Deposits Made		+$200.00
Withdrawals		-$326.00
Service Charge		-$ 5.00
Ending Balance as of	06/14/23	$245.40

BANK STATEMENTS AND RECONCILIATION

```
                         **DEPOSITS**
    DATE-----------AMOUNT
    05/24              100.00
    06/10              100.00


                         **WITHDRAWALS**
    NUMBER--DATE ----------AMOUNT
     135    05/16        $64.51
     136    05/17        $35.20
     137    05/24        $ 9.54
    CASH    05/26        $20.00
     138    05/29        $40.00
     139    06/02        $12.00
     141    06/09        $49.75
    CASH    06/12        $40.00
     142    06/14        $55.00
```

You can choose to have your bank statement arrive as a paper document, or be viewed online. In either case, you can see all the checks that the bank received (here called withdrawals since the money is withdrawn, or taken out, of your account) and the deposits you made during this period. There is usually a bank service charge for the handling of the account, and this is listed on the statement as well.

Balance is the amount of money in the account. The beginning balance is what you started with for the given period, and the ending balance is what is actually in the account at the end of the period.

An important thing to know is that the dates on the deposits and withdrawals are not necessarily the dates that you made them. For example, if you write a check on the 14th of the month, it may not get to the bank until the 17th, and the withdrawal would be listed on the 17th.

Notice that some of the withdrawals are labeled CASH. These are withdrawals made from ATMs (automatic teller machines), where it wasn't necessary to write a check (you punch in a number to identify yourself and then can take out cash from your account directly through the machine).

RECONCILIATION

Reconciliation means to bring two different things to be the same or equal. For example, farmer Jones is charging $7.00 for a box of apples. Neighbor Smith only wants to pay $3.00 for a box of apples. These numbers are different and may be reconciled by farmer Jones agreeing to sell the apples for $5.00 and neighbor Smith agreeing to buy them for that much.

With regards to your checking account, you are trying to reconcile the ending balance given in your statement with the amount that your checkbook shows that you currently have—also called "balancing" your checkbook. These may be different for several reasons:

1. Not all the checks you wrote may have gotten to the bank before the statement was completed. For example, notice that check #140 is not listed in the statement above. It was written, but for some reason hasn't arrived at the bank yet. So, it would have been subtracted from the balance on your stub, but the bank has not subtracted it from your account balance.

2. Not all the deposits you made have been recorded by the time the statement was completed.

3. The bank subtracts a service charge that you may not have noted on your stubs.

4. You or the bank have made an error. It may be that you failed to enter some transaction (such as a deposit or cash withdrawal) into your checkbook. Perhaps you didn't copy an amount correctly onto the stub or made an error in addition or subtraction. Or the bank may have made a mistake.

Let's see what a reconciliation of the above statement might look like.

BANK STATEMENTS AND RECONCILIATION

Suppose John Doe had kept a good record of his checks and deposits on his stubs, and in addition to the checks shown on the statement he had a record of these checks and deposits:

#	Date Written	Amount
140	5 June	$200
143	16 June	$50
Dep.	16 June	$100

The balance in his checkbook is $160.40. This is obviously different from the bank's account balance of $245.40.

The account balance and his checkbook balance may differ for any of the above four reasons, so to reconcile them he must take those into account.

First, John starts with the bank's account balance. He would add any deposits he has made which are not shown on the statement:

BANK BALANCE	CHECKBOOK BALANCE
$245.40	$160.40
+100.00	
$345.40	

Then he would subtract checks he has written which are not shown on the statement. In this case he has written a total of $250 in checks.

BANK BALANCE	CHECKBOOK BALANCE
$245.40	$160.40
+100.00	
$345.40	
−250.00	
$95.40	

Now he must subtract the service charge from his checkbook balance:

BANK BALANCE	CHECKBOOK BALANCE
$245.40	$160.40
+100.00	−5.00
$345.40	$155.40
−250.00	
$95.40	

The figures are not yet reconciled. Since we've taken care of the first three causes for difference, the problem must be an error. Can you see it? (Try to figure it out before you read on.)

The problem is that John didn't note in his checkbook the cash withdrawals he had made through the ATM. John would then adjust his checkbook by recording and subtracting from his checkbook balance the cash withdrawals he had forgotten to record earlier.

BANK BALANCE	CHECKBOOK BALANCE
$245.40	$160.40
+100.00	−5.00
$345.40	$155.40
−250.00	−60.00
$95.40	$95.40

Now the two figures match, and the statement has been reconciled to the checkbook. In other words, the account balances.

As you can see, it's important that you keep track of the current balance of your account, and any cash withdrawals or checks you've written so that you don't try to take out more money than is there.

BANK STATEMENTS AND RECONCILIATION

If this happens, there can be two penalties:

1. the bank doesn't pay the check, so the person you've written the check to doesn't get their money;

2. the bank then charges you a penalty, and takes the penalty amount directly out of your account, further reducing the money you thought you had.

ERRORS THAT CAN AFFECT RECONCILIATION

The purpose of reconciliation is to make sure there are no errors, since errors could cost you money. In addition to those mentioned above, here are some examples of errors that could affect your reconciliation.

1. You've written your check in pencil, and the person the check is made out to (or someone who took it) changed the amount, taking more out of your account. Using non-erasable pens will prevent this.

2. Numbers aren't written clearly, and the numeral "$_____" amount doesn't match the written "_____ Dollars" amount. Banks will reject items that are unreadable or show different amounts.

3. The check made out to you that you're attempting to deposit isn't accepted by the bank because the name signed on the back of the check doesn't match the name as written on the front.

CHAPTER 7

Reconciliation Practice

CHAPTER 7

Reconciliation Practice

Here are a set of stubs, a printed bank statement, and the checks and deposit slips that go along with the statement.

The checkbook balance is given on the last stub.

Reconcile the statement to the checkbook.

STUBS:

```
No. 155  $ 25.56
Date April 7   20 23
To:   Corner Store

For:  Food


Bal For'd    545|78
Amt Dep. _____
Total        545|78
This check    25|56
New Bal      520|22
```

```
No. 156  $ 42.35
Date April 9   20 23
To:   Electric
      Company
For:  March
      electric bill

Bal For'd    520|22
Amt Dep. _____
Total        520|22
This check    42|35
New Bal      477|87
```

RECONCILIATION PRACTICE

```
No. 157  $ 70.00
Date April 9   20 23
To:   Phone Co.

For:  April bill


Bal For'd   477 | 87
Amt Dep.
Total       477 | 87
This check   70 | 00
New Bal     407 | 87
```

```
No. 158  $ 45.78
Date April 10  20 23
To:   Doctor J.

For:  Exam


Bal For'd   407 | 87
Amt Dep.
Total       407 | 87
This check   45 | 78
New Bal     362 | 09
```

```
No. 159  $ 10.00
Date April 15  20 23
To:   Hobby store

For:  Model


Bal For'd   362 | 09
Amt Dep.     60 | 00
Total       422 | 09
This check   10 | 00
New Bal     412 | 09
```

```
No. 160  $ 15.65
Date April 29  20 23
To:   Corner store

For:  Food


Bal For'd   412 09
Amt Dep.
Total       412 09
This check   15 65
New Bal     396 44
```

```
JOHN DOE                                              155
JANE DOE                                         12-121/5555
123 Maple Dr.              April 7 20 23
Elmville, MA 13579

Pay to the
Order of      Corner Store                   $  25.56
     Twenty-five and 56/100--------------------  DOLLARS
        BANK OF MASSACHUSETTS
           Elmville, Massachusetts
Memo   food                        (signature)
*"13141592654*     :220141  3340455
```

RECONCILIATION PRACTICE

```
JOHN DOE                                                    156
JANE DOE                                                12-121/5555
123 Maple Dr.                         April 9  20 23
Elmville, MA 13579

Pay to the
Order of____Electric Co._____    $  42.35
    Forty-two and 35/100-----------------------    DOLLARS
       BANK OF MASSACHUSETTS
       Elmville, Massachusetts
Memo__bill_____                      _____(signature)_____
*"13141592654*       :220141  3340455
```

```
JOHN DOE                                                    157
JANE DOE                                                12-121/5555
123 Maple Dr.                         April 9  20 23
Elmville, MA 13579

Pay to the
Order of____Phone Co._____     $  70.00
    Seventy and no/100-------------------------    DOLLARS
       BANK OF MASSACHUSETTS
       Elmville, Massachusetts
Memo____bill_____                    _____(signature)_____
*"13141592654*       :220141  3340455
```

```
JOHN DOE                                                    158
JANE DOE                                                12-121/5555
123 Maple Dr.                         April 10  20 23
Elmville, MA 13579

Pay to the
Order of____Dr. J_____      $  45.78
    Forty-five and 78/100---------------------    DOLLARS
       BANK OF MASSACHUSETTS
       Elmville, Massachusetts
Memo_____exam____                    _____(signature)_____
*"13141592654*       :220141  3340455
```

RECONCILIATION PRACTICE

```
JOHN DOE                                              159
JANE DOE                                        12-121/5555
123 Maple Dr.                   April 15  20 23
Elmville, MA 13579

Pay to the
Order of_____Hobby store_____  $ 10.00
    Ten and no/100--------------------------------  DOLLARS
         BANK OF MASSACHUSETTS
            Elmville, Massachusetts
Memo____model____                    (signature)
*"13141592654*       :220141  3340455
```

DEPOSIT SLIPS:

Bank of Massachusetts	
Name: John Doe	
Acct. No. 22-3340455	
Date: April 15, 2023	
CASH	20|00
CHECKS	
	40|00
TOTAL	60|00

Bank of Massachusetts	
Name: John Doe	
Acct. No. 22-3340455	
Date: April 23, 2023	
CASH	
CHECKS	
	25|00
	35|00
TOTAL	60|00

RECONCILIATION PRACTICE

STATEMENT:

```
                    BANK OF MASSACHUSETTS
                      Statement of Account

   John Doe                              Bank of Massachusetts
   Jane Doe                              777 E. 7th Street
   123 Maple Dr.                         Elmville, MA  13578
   Elmville, MA  13579                   (508) 876-5432

              SUMMARY OF CHECKING ACCOUNT 3340455

   Beginning Balance as of      04/01/23            $545.78
   Deposits Made                                    $120.00
   Withdrawals                                      $193.69
   Service Charge                                   $  5.00
   Ending Balance as of         04/31/23            $467.09

                          **DEPOSITS**

   DATE--------------AMOUNT            DATE--------------AMOUNT

   4/15            60.00               04/24           60.00

                         **WITHDRAWALS**

   NUMBER—DATE------------AMOUNT       NUMBER—DATE------------AMOUNT

   155    04/09        $25.56          158    04/16        $45.78
   156    04/12        $42.35          159    04/19        $10.00
   157    04/12        $70.00
```

CHAPTER 8

Online Banking

CHAPTER 8

Online Banking

Online banking is a service offered by many financial institutions. Online banking can be offered by the local bank where you have your account, while some financial institutions are set up only for online banking. With online banking, a customer accesses their checking or savings account via the internet using a device such as a smartphone, tablet or computer.

With online banking, you can do anything you do at your local bank, as well as set up bills for payment, and view your account in real time. You can tell almost immediately what money has gone out and your current balance, allowing you to manage your money better.

This is helpful if you have set up direct deposits for money coming in, such as for paychecks or tax refunds, where the money goes directly into the account without going to you first to make the deposit. And it's especially important if you are using cash and/or a card to pay for many purchases rather than checks. (See the next chapter.)

You can choose to get your bank statements by mail or view them online.

Use of your online account requires a login name, and password. A disadvantage of online banking is the possibility of someone going into your account if they get access to your login name and password. Keeping both of these safe, and changing your password every so often can prevent this from happening.

CHAPTER 9

Debit and Credit Cards

CHAPTER 9

Debit and Credit Cards

Both debit and credit cards are cards with bank information that give you access to money, and can often be used instead of cash or a check. Here is how they are different:

- A debit card is tied to your bank account and uses money from that account.

- A credit card, even one issued by the same bank, uses money you borrow.

Let's see how each works.

DEBIT CARD

A debit card is tied to a bank account, and it can be used to withdraw and deposit money there, and to make purchases at stores. The amount of money that can be used is limited by the balance in the account. By inserting the debit card into an automated teller machine (ATM), and punching in a secret personal identification number (PIN), a deposit can be made, and money can be taken from the account as long as there are sufficient funds available.

With a debit card one can buy things without having to write a check; simply swipe or tap the card and enter the PIN on the keypad. Some stores allow a customer to get additional cash back from a purchase. For example, an item costs $12.75 and it asks on the keypad whether the customer wants cash back, and how much. The customer says they want $20 back, so $32.75 is taken from the account with $12.75 going to the store and $20 to the customer.

DEBIT AND CREDIT CARDS

Some stores don't take checks because there are people who write checks for money they don't have (called "bad checks") and the store is unable to collect. Stores will take a debit card because the money goes immediately into their account.

The customer's bank statement will show deposits made, checks that have gone through, where a debit card was used and the amount, and where an ATM was used and the amount, plus any fees. For reconciling a statement, it's important to keep track of all receipts/activities involving a debit card. Here is where having an online account is helpful as you can check on what money has gone in and out of your account as often as you wish.

CREDIT CARD

Because a credit card uses borrowed money, let's first take a look at how borrowing money works in general.

Maybe you've borrowed money from your parents to do, or buy, something you wanted. Your parents loaned you the money with the agreement that you would pay them back over some period of time; maybe they even charged you a "fee" or "interest" for the use of their money.

Financial institutions loan money in several ways. One way involves loaning a set amount of money, with the principal amount plus interest to be paid in monthly installments until it's paid in full. (Notice that this is the opposite of what happens when you give your money to an institution for a period of time and earn interest from them. In this case, the institution is letting you use their money—the principal—for a period of time, and they are earning interest from you.)

Here's an example: You fill out an application for a loan from a bank for $1,000. The bank looks at your income and **credit history** (how well you've kept your past payment agreements), and approves the loan. A loan agreement is made up for you to sign which gives the amount you are borrowing, the interest rate, and the monthly payments. In this case, the agreement states you are borrowing $1,000 at an interest rate of 20%. You will make monthly payments of $100 to pay back the principal plus interest ($1200) in one year. Once the money is paid back, the agreement is over. If you want to borrow more money, you fill out a new application for a loan. This is similar to the example of borrowing money from your parents.

A credit card is another tool a financial institution has for loaning money.

To get a credit card, a person fills out an application, and based on their income and credit history, they receive a card with a credit limit. This means, they can use this card to pay for various purchases up to the credit limit. At the end of the month, they can pay the entire balance, a partial balance or at least an agreed-upon minimum amount. Interest is charged on any amount left owing at the end of the month.

For example, Su Lin has a credit card with a credit limit of $2,000. This means she can borrow up to $2,000 using her card. She uses her credit card to buy two electric scooters for $800 each—one for herself and one for her brother. This means the bank has now loaned her $1600, and that balance is on her credit card account. At the end of the month, she has to pay at least the minimum amount, which is $80.00. And she will be charged interest by the bank on any remaining balance.

On the surface, this can seem very handy—and it is. Instead of having to make separate applications for loans, you have your credit card available for instant borrowing. However, it's important to understand exactly how this works, so you don't end up paying a lot more than you planned in interest. Remember, banks wouldn't offer credit cards if the credit cards didn't make them money.

Banks make their money on the interest they get. So, it's actually not ideal for them if people pay off the whole balance on their credit cards every month. Then the banks make no interest. So, if Su Lin paid off the whole $1600 at the end of the month, she doesn't have to pay interest, and the bank makes nothing from the fact that they lent her $1600 for 30 days. This is great for Su Lin and not so great for the bank.

DEBIT AND CREDIT CARDS

Banks want people to charge higher amounts on their credit cards, which makes it more likely they will "carry a balance," which means not pay the balance off each month. One way banks do this is to require only very small minimum payments. This encourages borrowers to buy more expensive things because they can afford the minimum payments. However, if they don't think with the amount of interest they are going to have to pay by carrying the balance, they can end up paying far more in interest than for the original purchase!

Because this practice caused many people to get so far into debt that they were unable to get out of it, institutions are now required to put a "warning" on monthly credit card statements. This warning states how long it will take to pay off the balance if only minimum payments are made, and how much the borrower will end up paying in the end. Here's an example:

Minimum Payment Warning: If you have a Balance and make only the minimum payment each period, you will pay more in interest and it will take you longer to pay off your Balance.

New Balance $1,450.82
Minimum Payment Due   40.00

If you make no additional charges and each month you pay…	You will pay off the balance shown on this statement in about…	And you will pay an estimated total of …
Only the Minimum Payment Due	5 years	$2,394
$55	3 years	$1,991 (Savings - $403)

It's easy to see how you will pay less money if you pay more than the minimum balance, or better yet the full balance, each month.

Remember, a debit card only uses money that is available in the bank account. A credit card, on the other hand, is a loan—a debt that the person owes. And depending on how well they manage it, it can be a useful tool or a tremendous burden.

CHAPTER 10

You Decide

CHAPTER 10

You Decide

You've learned that

- Money is something people agree has value. It can be exchanged more easily than objects for things, and you want to have more money than you need, not less.

- Planning and following a budget will help put you in control of your finances, and can keep you making more money than you spend.

- You can use money you are saving to make more money. There are different ways to do this. To help you decide, consider the rate of interest and the method by which it is computed, as well as the safety of your money.

- Inflation acts to reduce the value of money saved so you need to earn more than the rate of inflation to increase your buying power.

- Keeping good records of money in and money out of a checking (or savings) account ensures you can track and control spending.

- Debit and credit cards differ, with credit cards having the potential to keep you in debt and paying more money. You will pay less money to use a credit card if you pay more than the minimum balance, or even the entire balance, each month.

These are all good things to know, and are part of making good financial decisions. Using tools that lead to having more money than you need are up to you. You decide!